STRUCTURED INTERVIEWS:

A PRACTICAL GUIDE

U.S. Office of Personnel Management
Theodore Roosevelt Building
1900 E Street, NW
Washington, DC 20415-0001

September 2008

TABLE OF CONTENTS

Introduction

Overview

Federal Agency mission accomplishment is substantially affected by who gets hired. Agencies must select people who possess characteristics required for the job. The employment interview is an effective way of determining who has these attributes and therefore, who is right for a job.

The interview is popular because it is more personal than traditional selection assessments (e.g., written tests) and because it can be used to evaluate job characteristics not easily measured with other procedures (e.g., Oral Communication and Interpersonal Skills).

Interviews are typically used for one of two purposes in the Federal Government. First, the interview may be used as part of the formal selection process in which candidates are screened or ranked based on their scores. Second, a "selecting official's interview" may be used to verify candidates' qualifications for a job after they have been rated using other assessment methods, but prior to making a hiring decision. In a selecting official's interview, candidates' responses are typically not scored.

Structured vs. Unstructured Interviews

Employment interviews can be either *structured* or *unstructured*. Generally speaking, structured interviews ensure candidates have equal opportunities to provide information and are assessed accurately and consistently.

Structured Interview

- All candidates are asked the same questions in the same order.
- All candidates are evaluated using a common rating scale.
- Interviewers are in agreement on acceptable answers.

Unstructured Interview

- Candidates may be asked different questions.
- A standardized rating scale is not required.
- Interviewers do not need to agree on acceptable answers.

At first glance, the unstructured interview appears attractive due to its loose framework, discretionary content, and conversational flow. Yet, these same features make this type of interview very subjective, which reduces its accuracy and invites legal challenges.

Research consistently indicates *unstructured* interviews have little value in predicting job performance. Unstructured interviews typically demonstrate:
- Low levels of **reliability** (rating consistency among interviewers).
- Low to moderate levels of **validity** (the extent to which the assessment method measures what it is intended to measure, e.g., job performance).

Besides adversely affecting the reliability and validity of the unstructured interview, the lack of standardization in interview procedure and questions also makes the unstructured interview susceptible to legal challenges (Terpstra, Mohamed, and Kethley 1999[1]; U.S. Merit Systems Protection Board, 2003[2]).

In comparison, *structured* interviews have demonstrated a high degree of reliability, validity, and legal defensibility. Therefore, because interviews used to make employment decisions are subject to the same legal and psychometric requirements as any written employment test or other assessment method, agencies are encouraged to use structured interviews. The benefits of consistently selecting quality candidates and reducing the risk of legal challenges far outweigh any costs of adding structure (e.g., additional time and expertise).

The selecting official's interview is likely to fall somewhere between structured and unstructured, as it may incorporate a consistent set of questions but is unlikely to be rated.

The Purpose of this Guide

This guide provides practical information on designing structured interviews. The guide discusses *why* interviews should have structure, *what* structure consists of, and *how* to conduct a structured interview. It also addresses the pros and cons of different types of interview questions and helpful/harmful interviewing techniques. Additionally, the guide provides practical tools for developing and implementing a structured interview. For step-by-step checklists for implementing and developing a structured interview, refer to Appendix A and Appendix B, respectively.

The guidance on developing and administering structured interviews applies to interviews formally rated as part of the assessment process, as well as those used by the selection official to verify a candidate's qualifications after he/she has been rated by other assessment procedures. However, since responses are typically not scored in a selecting official's interview, the information in this document related to developing and using rating scales may be of limited use for the selecting official's interview.

This guide is not intended to be exhaustive of the possible approaches to developing a structured interview, but to provide one effective method. Additional information on assessment methods is available in OPM's online Personnel Assessment and Selection Resource Center. Please see also The Uniform Guidelines on Employee Selection Procedures and the Delegated Examining Operations Handbook.

---

[1] Terpstra, D. E., Mohamed, A. A., & Kethley, R. B. (1999). An analysis of Federal court cases involving nine selection devices. *International Journal of Selection and Assessment, 7,* 26-34.

[2] U. S. Merit Systems Protection Board. (2003). *The federal selection interview: Unrealized potential.* Washington, DC: Office of Policy and Evaluation.

Section I: Developing a Structured Interview

There are **8 key steps** in developing a structured interview. Appendix B provides a checklist based on these steps.

1. **Conduct a Job Analysis**
2. **Determine the Competencies to be Assessed by the Interview**
3. **Choose the Interview Format and Develop Questions**
4. **Develop Rating Scales to Evaluate Candidates**
5. **Create Interview Probes**
6. **Pilot-Test the Interview Questions**
7. **Create the Interviewer's Guide**
8. **Document the Development Process**

1. Conduct a Job Analysis

The purpose of a job analysis is to identify the requirements of the job and the competencies necessary to perform them. In many instances, a new job analysis will not need to be conducted; however, the critical requirements and competencies should be re-confirmed by subject matter experts. A thorough job analysis will:

- Identify the job tasks and responsibilities.
- Identify the competencies required to successfully perform the job tasks and responsibilities.
- Identify which of those competencies are required upon entry to the job.

To gather this information about a job, consider sources such as:

- Performance appraisal critical elements
- Position descriptions
- Classification standards
- Task statements
- Interviews with subject matter experts (e.g., high-performing employees, supervisors)
- Organizational charts

Chapter 2 and Appendix G of the Delegated Examining Operations Handbook provide additional information and tools for conducting a job analysis.

2. Determine the Competencies to be Assessed by the Interview

After identifying the critical competencies, determine which will be assessed in the selection process and how each competency will be measured (e.g., using a written test or interview). OPM's interactive Assessment Decision Tool provides suggested methods for assessing a range of competencies and also provides evaluation criteria for each assessment method.

The structured interview is typically used to assess between four and six competencies, unless the job is unique or at a high level. Some competencies (e.g., Oral Communication, Interpersonal Skills) are particularly well-suited to assessment through an interview.

3. Choose the Interview Format and Develop Questions

The format of the interview can focus on candidates' past behavior, their anticipated behavior in hypothetical situations, or a combination of the two approaches. An interview based on questions about past behaviors is a behavioral description interview, also known as a behavioral event interview. An interview based on questions about hypothetical behavior is a situational interview. In the remainder of this document, "behavioral interview" will refer to both the behavioral description interview and the behavioral event interview.

The interview format will determine how the interview questions are developed. The two interview formats measure different aspects of job performance. Therefore, deciding which format to use depends upon the needs and resources of the agency and on the other assessments used. The agency may elect to include questions derived from both the behavioral- and situational-interview formats.

Regardless of the format, the interview questions should be:

- Reflective of competencies derived from a job analysis
- Realistic of the responsibilities of the job
- Open-ended
- Clear and concise
- At a reading level appropriate for the candidates
- Free of jargon

Behavioral Interview Format and Questions. The primary purpose of the behavioral interview is to gather information from job candidates about their *actual* behavior during *past* experiences which demonstrates competencies required for the job. The underlying premise is the best predictor of future behavior on the job is past behavior under similar circumstances.

For example, consider the competency, Interpersonal Skills, defined as: "shows understanding, friendliness, courtesy, tact, empathy, concern, and politeness to others; develops and maintains effective relationships with others; may include effectively dealing with individuals who are difficult, hostile, or distressed; relates well to people from varied backgrounds and different situations; is sensitive to cultural diversity, race, gender, disabilities, and other individual differences." This definition could lead to a behavioral interview question focused on a candidate's past behavior such as:

> Describe a situation in which you dealt with individuals who were difficult, hostile, or distressed. Who was involved? What specific actions did you take and what was the result?

Writing Behavioral Interview Questions. Convene a group of approximately six or seven subject matter experts (SMEs). These SMEs should be experienced, high-performing employees or supervisors who possess knowledge of the job at the level of the position to be filled. Typically, SMEs are at the journey level or higher.

- Have SMEs familiarize themselves with the competencies (and their definitions) to be measured by the interview.
- Have SMEs work together to write interview questions.
    - Each question should measure at least one of the specified competencies.
    - Each question should be written to elicit *specific details* about a situation, task, or context, the actions the person took or did not take, and the impact of these actions.
- SMEs should use superlative adjectives in the questions (e.g., most, last, worst, least) to help the candidate focus on specific incidents.
- SMEs should develop more questions than are actually needed to allow for subsequent discarding of questions during review and tryout.

Situational Interview Format and Questions. In contrast to the behavioral interview, the questions in a situational interview are based on future-oriented behavior. Situational interview questions give the candidate realistic job scenarios or dilemmas and ask how he/she *would* respond. The underlying premise is a person's intentions are closely tied to his/her actual behavior.

An example situational interview question for the competency Interpersonal Skills is:

> A very angry client walks up to your desk. She says she was told your office sent her an overdue check five days ago. She claims she has not received the check. She says she has bills to pay, and no one will help her. How would you handle this situation?

Writing Situational Interview Questions. Typically, the *critical incident method*, outlined below, is used to write situational interview questions (Flanagan, 1954)[3].

- Assemble a group of subject matter experts (SMEs) who have extensive knowledge about the job.
- Have the SMEs review the competencies (and their definitions) to be measured by the interview and the job tasks linked to the competencies.
- Have SMEs write examples of effective and ineffective behaviors (i.e., critical incidents) which reflect the competencies and associated tasks.
- Arrange for a separate group of SMEs to read each critical incident and identify the competency they believe the incident best illustrates.
    - This will confirm whether the critical incidents can be clearly linked to the specific competencies to which they are supposed to be linked.

---

[3] Flanagan, J. C. (1954). The critical incident technique. *Psychological Bulletin, 51*, 327-358.

- o Eliminate critical incidents not clearly linked to a competency and those associated with multiple competencies.
- Have SMEs rewrite the retained critical incidents in the form of hypothetical situations.
  - o These hypothetical situations should still demonstrate the correct competency.
  - o The hypothetical situations should be as real as possible and reflective of the job.
- As with the behavioral interview, have SMEs develop more questions than are actually needed to allow for future elimination.

Appendix C provides example forms for writing critical incidents describing effective and ineffective behavior.

4. Developing Rating Scales to Evaluate Candidates

NOTE: This step is not applicable to a selecting official's interview.

The use of a common rating scale for all candidates is a key component of the structured interview procedure. A standardized rating scale can be developed for either behavioral- or situational-interview questions; however, the process is slightly different.

Rating Scale and Behavioral Examples for a Behavioral Interview. The first step in the development of a standardized rating scale for a behavioral interview is specifying the range of proficiency for each competency.

- Decide on *one* proficiency-level range for all competencies (e.g., a range of 1-5 with 5 being the most proficient and 1 being the least proficient).
- Create at least three proficiency levels, but aim for five to seven levels.
- Label at least three proficiency levels (e.g., unsatisfactory, satisfactory, and superior).

Table 1 provides a 5-level proficiency rating scale developed by OPM. Labels are provided for each of the five levels.

Table 1: Rating Scale

Proficiency Level	General Competencies	Technical Competencies
Level 5 - Expert	<ul><li>Applies the competency in exceptionally difficult situations.</li><li>Serves as a key resource and advises others.</li></ul>	<ul><li>Applies the competency in exceptionally difficult situations.</li><li>Serves as a key resource and advises others.</li><li>Demonstrates comprehensive, expert understanding of concepts and processes.</li></ul>
Level 4 - Advanced	<ul><li>Applies the competency in considerably difficult situations.</li><li>Generally requires little or no guidance.</li></ul>	<ul><li>Applies the competency in considerably difficult situations.</li><li>Generally requires little or no guidance.</li><li>Demonstrates broad understanding of concepts and processes.</li></ul>

Proficiency Level	General Competencies	Technical Competencies
Level 3 - Intermediate	• Applies the competency in difficult situations. • Requires occasional guidance.	• Applies the competency in difficult situations. • Requires occasional guidance. • Demonstrates understanding of concepts and processes.
Level 2 - Basic	• Applies the competency in somewhat difficult situations. • Requires frequent guidance.	• Applies the competency in somewhat difficult situations. • Requires frequent guidance. • Demonstrates familiarity with concepts and processes.
Level 1 - Awareness	• Applies the competency in the simplest situations. • Requires close and extensive guidance.	• Applies the competency in the simplest situations. • Requires close and extensive guidance. • Demonstrates awareness of concepts and processes.

For a behavioral interview, develop example behaviors for *each proficiency level of each competency.* The purpose of these example behaviors is to clearly differentiate between proficiency levels for each competency. This will ease the rating process by giving interviewers concrete behaviors to refer to as they are considering how proficient each candidate is on each competency. The example behaviors will provide a common framework for assessing candidates' responses in a consistent manner.

Subject matter experts (SMEs) should assist in developing the behavioral examples for each behavioral interview question.

- Reconvene the panel of SMEs who developed the behavioral interview questions.
- For each question, have SMEs individually determine how actual employees at each proficiency level would respond (i.e., what their answers would be).
  - o These hypothetical responses are behavioral examples for the proficiency levels.
- Have the SMEs discuss their behavioral examples.
- For each proficiency level, retain behavioral examples which the SMEs agree best reflect the competency at that level.
- Instruct interviewers to use these behavioral examples as a *general guide* (not an absolute) in making their ratings, as candidate's responses may differ depending on their unique experiences (Feild and Gatewood, 1989)[4].

Table 2 presents an example behavioral interview rating scale for a question based on the competency Interpersonal Skills. This rating scale has been supplemented with behavioral examples to illustrate differences between the proficiency levels.

---

[4] Feild, H. S., & Gatewood, R. D. (1989). Development of a selection interview: A job content strategy. In Eder, R. W. & Ferris, G. R. (Eds.), *The employment interview: Theory, research, and practice* (pp. 145-157). Newbury Park, California: Sage Publications.

Table 2: Example of a Behavioral Interview Question and Rating Scale

Competency: Interpersonal Skills
Definition: Shows understanding, friendliness, courtesy, tact, empathy, concern, and politeness to others; develops and maintains effective relationships with others; may include effectively dealing with individuals who are difficult, hostile, or distressed; relates well to people from varied backgrounds and different situations; is sensitive to cultural diversity, race, gender, disabilities, and other individual differences.
Question: Describe a situation in which you had to deal with individuals who were difficult, hostile, or distressed. Who was involved? What specific actions did you take and what was the result?

Proficiency Level	Definition	Question-Specific Behavioral Examples
Level 5 Expert	• Applies the competency in exceptionally difficult situations. • Serves as a key resource and advises others.	• Presents shortcomings of a newly installed HR automation system in a tactful manner to irate senior management officials. • Explains the benefits of controversial policy changes to a group of upset individuals at a public hearing. • Diffuses an emotionally charged meeting with external stakeholders by expressing empathy for their concerns.
Level 4 Advanced	• Applies the competency in considerably difficult situations. • Generally requires little or no guidance.	• Facilitates an open forum to discuss employee concerns about a new compensation system. • Builds on the ideas of others to foster cooperation during bargaining agreement negotiations. • Identifies and emphasizes common goals to promote cooperation between HR and line staff. • Identifies and alleviates sources of stress among a team developing a new automated HR system.
Level 3 Intermediate	• Applies the competency in difficult situations. • Requires occasional guidance.	• Restores a working relationship between angry co-workers who have opposing views. • Remains courteous and tactful when confronted by an employee who is frustrated by a payroll problem. • Establishes cooperative working relationships with managers, so they are comfortable asking for advice on HR issues.
Level 2 Basic	• Applies the competency in somewhat difficult situations. • Requires frequent guidance.	• Offers to assist employees in resolving problems with their benefits election. • Works with other HR staff on a cross-functional team to improve coordination of activities. • Works with others to minimize disruptions to an employee working under tight deadlines.
Level 1 Awareness	• Applies the competency in the simplest situations. • Requires close and extensive guidance.	• Refers employees to the appropriate staff member to resolve their issues. • Works with others in the HR office to organize information for employee intervention sessions on controversial issues. • Works with others to obtain employee concerns about controversial policy changes.

Rating Scale and Behavioral Responses for a Situational Interview. As with behavioral interview questions, the first step in the development of a rating scale for each situational interview question is specifying the range of proficiency for each competency being assessed.

- Decide on *one* proficiency-level range for all competencies.
- Have at least three proficiency levels, but aim for five to seven levels.
- Provide labels for at least three proficiency levels (e.g., unsatisfactory, satisfactory, and superior).

Next, develop a representative response for each competency proficiency-level for each hypothetical job-scenario question. A representative response illustrates how someone with the given proficiency level on the given competency might behave. To develop the representative responses for proficiency levels of each situational interview question, follow these steps:

- Reconvene the panel of subject matter experts (SMEs) who developed the interview questions.
- For each hypothetical scenario, have each SME individually determine how actual employees at each proficiency level might behave (i.e., what their answers would be).
  - o These answers are representative responses for the proficiency-level ratings.
- Have the SMEs discuss their representative responses.
- For each proficiency level, retain the representative responses which the SMEs agree are the best.

Table 3 shows an example proficiency-level rating scale for a situational interview question with representative responses for each proficiency level. The situational interview question is derived from a job task and reflects a particular competency. This linkage needs to be present for all questions.

Table 3: Example of a Situational Interview Question and Rating Scale

Job Task	Competency	Interview Question	Proficiency Level & Representative Response
Performs investigative work to obtain information, gather evidence, or verify facts.	*Integrity/ Honesty:* Contributes to maintaining the integrity of the organization; displays high standards of ethical conduct and understands the impact violating these standards would have on an organization, self, and others; is trustworthy.	You are investigating a group of auto dealership managers suspected of money-laundering activities. During the course of an interview with one suspect, the suspect offers to help you buy a car at a price you know is well below market value. What would you do?	*Unsatisfactory:* Accept the offer.

Satisfactory: Say no to the offer and continue the investigation; document the incident in your report.

Superior: Probe the dealership managers to determine how they are able to offer a car at such a reduced price; attempt to get contact information of others involved; say no to the offer; and document the details of the incident. |

5. Create Interview Probes

A probe is a question asked by the interviewer to help clarify a candidate's response or ensure the candidate has provided enough information. When probes are necessary, interviewers should use very similar probes for all candidates to ensure candidates are given the same opportunities to excel. While probes may need to be tailored to address each candidate's specific response, the general meaning of the probes should not change.

- Prior to the interview, establish the desired range of probing (for example, no probes, a limited number of probes, unlimited probes).
- If probes will be used, determine the specific probes for each question the interviewer is allowed to use.

Example probes for behavioral- and situational-interview questions are presented in Table 4.

Table 4: Example Probes for Behavioral- and Situational-Interview Questions

Competency: Interpersonal Skills	
Behavioral Interview Question: Describe a situation in which you had to deal with individuals who were difficult, hostile, or distressed. Who was involved? What specific actions did you take and what was the result?	**Behavioral Interview Probes:** **Situation** • What factors led up to the situation? • Could you or anyone else have done something to prevent the situation? • What did you determine as the most critical issue to address in this situation? **Action** • How did you respond? • What was the most important factor you considered in taking action? • What is the first thing you did? **Outcome** • What was the outcome? • Is there anything you would have said and/or done differently? • Were there any benefits from the situation?
Situational Interview Question: A very angry client walks up to your desk. She says she was told your office sent her an overdue check five days ago. She claims she has not received the check. She says she has bills to pay, and no one will help her. How would you handle this situation?	**Situational Interview Probes:** **Situation** • Why do you believe this situation occurred? • What do you consider the most critical issue in this situation? • What other issues are of concern? **Action** • What would you say? • What is the first thing you would do? • What factors would affect your course of action? • What other actions could you take? **Outcome** • How do you think your action would be received? • What would you do if your action was not received well? • What do you consider as benefits of your action?

6. Pilot Test the Interview Questions and Evaluate the Interview Process

Prior to using the newly developed behavioral interview and/or situational interview questions in an actual interview, give the questions to colleagues for a trial run. This trial run (i.e., pilot test) will ensure questions are clearly worded and draw an appropriate range of responses. The pilot test will indicate if and where revisions need to be made. To the extent possible, the pilot test should mirror the actual structured interview.

7. Create the Interviewer's Guide

After finalizing the questions and rating scales, create an interviewer's guide. The interviewer's guide should provide general instructions about the interview process, a summary of common rating biases and rating mistakes to avoid, and general tips for good interviewing (see Section II). The guide should also provide information specific to the particular interview, including:

- Definitions of each competency being assessed
- Proficiency levels of each competency
- Interview questions
- Rating scale (with behavioral examples and/or representative responses) for each question
- Example probes

8. Document the Development Process

You should maintain records of the entire interview development process, in accordance with the Delegated Examining Operations Handbook. The documentation should include:

- Descriptions of all participants, including subject matter experts and those in the pilot study (e.g., name, job title, race, national origin, sex, and level of expertise).
- Interview development materials (e.g., reference materials, previous manuals).
- A description of the development of the interview, including the job analysis, the question and rating scale development process, and the pilot test.

Section II: Administering a Structured Interview

Interviewers

In Federal Agencies, interviews are typically conducted by one person, namely the selecting official (i.e., supervisor) for the position being filled. While the following sections are directed toward the use of one interviewer, a structured interview may also be administered by a *panel* of interviewers. A typical panel consists of two or more persons who have extensive knowledge of the job and are trained in administering interviews.

For information on using a panel to conduct the structured interview, please refer to Appendix D.

Training Your Interviewer

It is essential to train the person who will administer the structured interview. Interviewer training increases the accuracy of the interview. Before or during the training, the interviewer should receive a guide describing the interview process in detail.

Appendix E provides a sample lesson plan for an interviewer training course. The training should emphasize the importance of note-taking, discuss the impact of the interviewer's non-verbal behavior, and review common rating biases and errors.

Note-Taking. Taking regular and detailed notes of observable behaviors and verbal responses during each interview is crucial. Notes will reduce the burden on the interviewer to remember details about multiple candidates. Additionally, these notes should:

- Summarize the content and delivery of respondents' answers.
- Document the candidate's grammar, body language, and other non-verbal factors.
- Help interviewers focus on pertinent information during the interview.
- Be of sufficient quality and quantity to document the interviewer's reasoning for each rating on each competency.
- Serve as documentation to support the employment decision.

Interviewer's Non-Verbal Behavior. An interviewer's body language such as facial expressions and body movements (e.g., nodding, raising eyebrows, frowning) communicates a lot to the candidate. For example, the interviewer communicates disinterest by slouching, regularly looking at the clock, leaning back, or doodling with a pen.

Interviewers need be aware of their body language to avoid communicating negative impressions. Additionally, while taking notes, interviewers should make periodic eye contact with the candidate to show their interest and to provide opportunities to observe the candidate's non-verbal behavior.

Interpersonal Bias and Rating Errors. Bias and rating errors are inconsistent with the purpose of the structured interview process, namely, ensuring candidates are evaluated fairly, consistently, and have equal opportunities to excel. The interviewer should not be influenced by personal biases or fall prey to common rating errors.

Biases can take a variety of forms. For example, an interviewer might give higher ratings to candidates who appear outwardly similar to him/her. *Rating errors* might include giving all high ratings or all low ratings to candidates. Appendix F describes common rating errors and interviewing mistakes.

The Interview Setting

The interview should take place in a comfortable environment.

- Interviews should be held in a quiet, non-threatening, and private place.
- Seating arrangements should be the same for all candidates.
- The interview room and facilities must be accessible to candidates with disabilities.
- There should be a separate area for those waiting to be interviewed.
- Individuals who have been interviewed should not be allowed to communicate with those waiting to be interviewed.
- Interviews should be scheduled far enough in advance to provide adequate preparation time for the interviewer.
- All candidates should be allotted the same amount of interview time.

Conducting the Interview

Supplemental Materials. While candidates may be permitted to bring supplemental documents to the interview (e.g., references, transcripts, or a resume), this information is for the *candidate's reference only* and should not be looked at by the interviewer during the interview. Allowing interviewers to look at these documents during the interview may bias the interviewer's perceptions of the candidates (e.g., interviewers might rate the responses of candidates with strong resumes more favorably then those of candidates with weak resumes). If interviewers look at supplemental information during the interview and this supplemental information is not provided by all candidates, candidates may be evaluated inconsistently.

Arrival of the Candidate.

- Welcome the candidate in a warm and friendly manner.
- Thank the candidate for his/her interest in the position and for coming to the interview.
- Briefly describe the job and relevant organizational characteristics to allow candidates to become comfortable in the interview setting.
- Explain the interview process in a standardized way. You may also provide this information in writing to each candidate.
- Inform the candidate that notes will be taken throughout the interview.
- Ask the candidate if he/she has any questions before beginning.

At the end of the interview, the interviewer should ask, "Is there anything else you would like us to know?" and provide the candidate with an opportunity to ask questions. The interviewer should then thank and excuse the candidate.

Rating Each Candidate. Immediately after the candidate leaves the room, the interviewer should review his or her notes and, if the interview is being rated, rate the candidate. Notes should include actual behavioral examples and ratings should be defensible and supported by the notes. Examples of actual answers given should be included along with explanations of how these answers apply to the competency being rated and why they merit the given rating. Examples of rating forms for use by one interviewer or a panel of interviewers can be found in Appendix G and Appendix H, respectively.

After all candidates have been rated, the interviewer should:

- Review the ratings given to each candidate.
- Ensure the total performance of each candidate has been considered thoroughly and objectively.
- Ensure the ratings are tied to specific behavioral examples.
- Sign and date each rating form.

Documenting the Interview Process

In addition to the documentation mentioned above, the following information should be recorded and retained:
- Date, time, place, and length of the interview
- Name, job title, race, national origin, and sex of the interviewer
- Interview questions, scores, and notes for each candidate
- Training provided to the interviewer
- Interview guides, rating scales, and other materials used

References

Campion, J. E., & Arvey, R. D. (1989). Unfair discrimination in the employment interview. In Eder, R. W. & Ferris, G. R. (Eds.), *The employment interview: Theory, research and practice* (pp. 61-73). Newbury Park, California: Sage Publications.

Campion, M. A., Campion, J. E., & Hudson, J. P. Jr. (1994). Structured interviewing: A note on incremental validity and alternative question types. *Journal of Applied Psychology, 79,* 998-1002.

Campion, M. A., Palmer, D. K., & Campion, J. E. (1997). A review of structure in the selection interview. *Personnel Psychology, 50,* 655-702.

Campion, M., Pursell, E., & Brown, B. (1988). Structured interviewing: Raising the psychometric properties of the employment interview. *Personnel Psychology, 41,* 25-42.

Cascio, W. F., & Aguinis, H. (2005). *Applied Psychology in Human Resource Management, 6th Edition.* New Jersey: Pearson Prentice Hall.

Conway, J. M., & Peneno, G. M. (1999). Comparing structured interview question types: Construct validity and candidate reactions. *Journal of Business and Psychology, 13,* 485-506.

Day, A. L., & Carroll, S. A. (2003). Situational and patterned behavior description interviews: A comparison of their validity, correlates, and perceived fairness. *Human Performance, 16,* 25-47.

Feild, H. S., & Gatewood, R. D. (1989). Development of a selection interview: A job content strategy. In Eder, R. W. & Ferris, G. R. (Eds.), *The employment interview: Theory, research, and practice* (pp. 145-157). Newbury Park, California: Sage Publications.

Flanagan, J. C. (1954). The critical incident technique. *Psychological Bulletin, 51,* 327-358.

Gael, S. (1984). *Job analysis: A guide to assessing work activities.* San Francisco: Jossey-Bass.

Harris, M. M. (1989). Reconsidering the employment interview: A review of recent literature and suggestions for future research. *Personnel Psychology, 42,* 691-726.

Huffcutt, A. I., Weekley, J. A., Wiesner, W. H., Degroot, T. G., & Jones, C. (2001). Comparison of situational and behavior description interview questions for higher-level positions. *Personnel Psychology, 54,* 619-644.

Janz, T. (1982). Initial comparisons of patterned behavior description interviews versus unstructured interviews. *Journal of Applied Psychology, 67,* 557-580.

Latham, G. P. & Saari, L. M. (1984). Do people do what they say? Further studies on the situational interview. *Journal of Applied Psychology, 69,* 569-573.

Latham, G. P., Saari, L. M., Pursell, E. D., & Campion, M. A. (1980). The situational interview. *Journal of Applied Psychology, 65,* 422-427.

Latham, G. P., & Sue-Chan, C. (1999). A meta-analysis of the situational interview: An enumerative review of reasons for its validity. *Canadian Psychology, 40,* 56-67.

Locke, E. A. (1968). Towards a theory of task motivation and incentives. *Organizational Behavior and Human Performance, 3,* 157-189.

McDaniel, M. A., Whetzel, D. L., Schmidt, F. L., & Maurer, S. D. (1994). The validity of employment interviews: A comprehensive review and meta-analysis. *Journal of Applied Psychology, 79,* 599-616.

Mento, A. J. (1980). *Suggestions for structuring and conducting the selection interview* (Professional Paper 80-1). Washington, DC: U. S. Office of Personnel Management, Personnel Research and Development Center.

Motowildo, S. J., Carter, G. W., Dunnett, M. D., Tippins, N., Werner, S., Burnett, J. R., & Vaughn, M. J. (1992). Studies of the structured behavioral interview. *Journal of Applied Psychology, 77,* 571-587.

Muldrow, T. W. (1987). *Developing and conducting interviews: Some general guidance.* Washington, DC: U. S. Office of Personnel Management.

Orpen, C. (1985). Patterned behavior description interviews versus unstructured interviews: A comparative validity study. *Journal of Applied Psychology, 70,* 774-776.

Outerbridge, A. N. (1994). *Developing and conducting the structured situational interview: A practical guide.* Washington, DC: U.S. Office of Personnel Management, Office of Personnel Research and Development, PRD-94-01.

Pulakos, E. D., & Schmitt, N. (1995). Experience-based and situational interview questions: Studies of validity. *Personnel Psychology, 48,* 289-308.

Schmidt, F. L., & Hunter, J. E. (1998). The validity and utility of selection methods in personnel psychology: Practical and theoretical implications of 85 years of research findings. *Psychological Bulletin, 124,* 262-274.

Terpstra, D. E., Mohamed, A. A., & Kethley, R. B. (1999). An analysis of Federal court cases involving nine selection devices. *International Journal of Selection and Assessment, 7,* 26-34.

U. S. Merit Systems Protection Board. (2003). *The federal selection interview: Unrealized potential.* Washington, DC: Office of Policy and Evaluation.

Whitley, B. E. (2002). *Principles of Research in Behavioral Science, 2ⁿᵈ Edition.* New York: McGraw-Hill.

Appendix A: Structured Interview Implementation Checklist

☐ **Assess the Current Selection Situation.** Discuss the need for developing a structured interview and the specific goals for the structured interview. Also determine which job or jobs will use the structured interview.

☐ **Determine Where the Structured Interview Fits within the Selection Process.** Determine where to place the structured interview in the selection of job candidates (e.g., after a written test, as the last selection procedure). Federal Agencies typically use the interview after candidates have been determined eligible for a given job and rated/ranked on the basis of other assessment tools (e.g., a written test or resume). The interview is then used to verify a candidate's qualifications.

☐ **Create a Development and Implementation Plan with Timelines.** Plan the major steps for developing the structured interview, including updating or conducting a job analysis, convening subject matter experts to develop the interview questions and rating scale, and training interviewers on how to evaluate candidates.

☐ **Ensure Compliance of the Plan with Established Guidelines.** Make sure the structured interview process complies with the requirements in The Uniform Guidelines on Employee Selection Procedures and the Delegated Examining Operations Handbook.

☐ **Create a Communication Plan and Obtain Commitment to the Plan.** Ensure managers are aware of the intent of the structured interview.

☐ **Establish Structured Interview Development Team(s).** Identify the development and implementation team, which may include human resources specialists, selecting officials, supervisors, and/or employees.

☐ **Develop the Structured Interview.** (See Appendix B: Structured Interview Development Checklist)

☐ **Administer the Structured Interview.**

☐ **Evaluate the Results.** Monitor the implementation of the structured interview on a periodic basis to ensure the plan is followed and the intended results are achieved. Adjust the structured interview procedure as necessary.

Appendix B: Structured Interview Development Checklist

☐ **1. Conduct a Job Analysis.** Identify the job characteristics (i.e., job tasks, duties, and responsibilities) and the competencies/knowledge, skills, abilities required to perform the job successfully.

☐ **2. Determine the Competencies to be Assessed by the Interview.** Consider which competencies are measured most effectively with an interview.

☐ **3. Choose the Interview Format and Develop Questions.** Determine if you will use a behavioral interview or situational interview. Work with subject matter experts to develop questions.

☐ **4. Develop Rating Scales to Evaluate Candidates.** Determine the proficiency scale and develop accompanying proficiency level examples. (NOTE: May not be applicable to a selecting official's interview.)

☐ **5. Create Interview Probes.** Establish if probes may be used. If probes will be used, draft specific probes for each question.

☐ **6. Pilot-Test the Interview Questions.** Pilot test the interview questions on persons similar to the anticipated candidates. Check for clarity and appropriateness.

☐ **7. Create the Interviewer's Guide.** Prepare an interviewer's guide, question booklet, and rating form.

☐ **8. Document the Development Process.** Document all stages of the interview development.

Appendix C: Sample Critical Incident Forms

Effective Incident Form
Job Title:
Competency:
Instructions: Think of an incident during the past year in which you were particularly proud of your performance, or the performance of a coworker, and share it with us. The incident must be related to performance on the job. The incident may have involved people, facilities, information, or another item relevant to performance on the job. Recalling this incident, please answer the following questions:
1. What circumstances led to the incident? (Situation)
2. What did you or your co-worker do that was very effective at the time? (Action)
3. Why was this incident very helpful in getting the job done? (Outcome)

Ineffective Incident Form
Job Title:
Competency:
Instructions: Think back over the past year and describe an incident that should have been handled differently. The incident must be related to your performance or the performance of a coworker on the job. The incident may have involved people, facilities, information, or another item relevant to performance on the job. Recalling the incident, please answer the following questions:
1. What circumstances led to the incident? (Situation)
2. What did you or your co-worker do that was ineffective at that time? (Action)
3. What were the effects of the actions? (Outcome)
4. What should have been done differently?

Appendix D: Panel Interviews

During the interview process, an abundance of information is exchanged between the candidate and the interviewer. A panel of two or three interviewers may be better able to document and interpret the information. A panel also reduces the risk of biases in ratings and allows for a diverse (e.g., race and sex) range of interviewers, indicating to the candidate that the organization values diversity and fair treatment.

Interviewers may conduct the interview together at one time or individually in a serial fashion in which the candidate progresses through multiple interviews. When feasible, the same interviewers should be used (either in a panel or serially) across all candidates, to ensure consistency in ratings.

In a panel interview, each panel member should individually observe, record, and evaluate the responses of the candidates. After each candidate, panel members should discuss their individual ratings. Final scores or ratings should be based on the consensus of the panel. This process is described in more detail below.

Although the interview panel works as a team, one panel member is typically designated as the chairperson or coordinator and he/she is responsible for the administrative and logistical arrangements of the interview and for documenting the process.

Conducting a Panel Interview

Before the candidate enters the interview room, the panel coordinator should verify all panel members understand the procedures to be followed and have all necessary materials. The interview process should be described in detail in the interviewer's guide and the guide should be provided to each panel member.

Upon each candidate's arrival, the panel coordinator should:

- Welcome the candidate and introduce each panel member.
- Thank the candidate for his/her interest in the position and for coming to the interview.
- Briefly describe the job and relevant organizational characteristics as to allow candidates to become comfortable in the interview setting.
- Explain the interview process in a standardized way. This explanation may also be provided to applicants in writing.
- Inform the candidate that notes will be taken throughout the interview.
- Ask if the candidate has any questions before beginning.

At the end of the interview, the coordinator should thank the candidate, answer any general questions, and excuse the candidate.

Making Candidate Ratings. Each panel member should **independently** review his/her notes immediately after the candidate leaves the room and, if the interview is not a selecting official's interview, rate the candidate. At this stage, each panelist is forming an independent evaluation without discussion with other panel members. Ratings should be specific, defensible, and supported by behavioral examples. Interviewers should include actual examples of answers given, explanations of how these answers apply to the competency being rated, and why they merit the given rating.

After panel members have independently rated all candidates, they should compare notes, ratings, and supporting observations. Panel members should thoroughly explore the basis for discrepancies in their ratings, and then reach a consensus on each candidate. Statements made by the candidate should be recorded to support specific ratings. Panelists should record the consensus rating for each candidate on a group rating form. Appendix H provides a sample group rating form.

After the last candidate has been rated, panelists should review the group ratings given to all candidates. This exchange will ensure the performance of each candidate has been considered thoroughly and objectively. This also ensures the final ratings represent the consensus judgment of the panel. After all ratings have been meticuously reviewed, they should be declared final and each member should attest to the final ratings by signing the group rating form.

Appendix E: Sample Lesson Plan for an Interviewer Training Course

Lesson 1: Introduction
- Interview Reliability and Validity
- Court Challenges and the Importance of adding Structure to the Interview Process
- Relationship of the Interview to the Total Hiring Process

Lesson 2: Interview Material
- General Interview Guidelines
- Awareness of Interviewer Biases and Mistakes
- Competency Definitions and Job Information
- Interview Questions (Behavior Interview or Situational Interview)
- Behavioral examples Responses
- Rating Forms and Procedures
- Sample Rating Forms

Lesson 3: Interview Process and Practice Exercises
- Interview Procedures
- Checklist of "Do's and Don'ts" for Conducting the Interview
- Critiqued Practice Using a Videotaped Interview
- Security of Interview Materials

Appendix F: Common Rating Errors and Interviewing Mistakes

Common Rating Errors

One way to minimize rating errors is to make interviewers aware of the most common types of error, which are summarized below.

1. **Rater Bias:** Allowing prejudices about certain groups of people or personalities to interfere with being able to fairly evaluate a candidate's performance. Interviewers should refrain from considering any non-performance related factors when making judgments.

2. **Halo Effect:** Allowing ratings of performance in one competency to influence ratings for other competencies. For example, allowing a high rating on Oral Communication to bias the rating on Problem Solving, irrespective of the candidate's performance on Problem Solving.

3. **Central Tendency:** A tendency to rate all competencies at the middle of the rating scale (for example, giving all "3s" on a 5-point scale). When hesitating over making a high rating, interviewers should realize such a rating does not indicate perfect performance; it means demonstrating more of the competency than is generally exhibited. Similarly, when hesitating over a low rating, interviewers should realize it does not mean the candidate does not possess the competency; it means he/she did not demonstrate much of the competency in his/her interview responses.

4. **Leniency:** A tendency to give high ratings to all candidates, irrespective of their actual performance. There may be candidates who could benefit from further development in certain areas. Interviewers should allow their ratings to reflect these intra- and inter-individual differences.

5. **Strictness:** A tendency to give low ratings to all candidates, irrespective of their actual performance. There may be outstanding candidates whose demonstration of competencies warrants high ratings. Interviewers should allow their ratings to reflect these intra- and inter-individual differences.

6. **Similar to Me:** Giving higher than deserved ratings to candidates who appear similar to you. People have a natural tendency to prefer others who are similar in various ways to themselves. Interviewers should concentrate on the responses given by the candidate in making evaluations, rather than on the outward characteristics and personality of the candidate.

Interviewers can minimize these rating errors by thoroughly understanding the competencies being assessed and by learning to compare the behaviors exhibited in the interview with the behaviors anchoring the proficiency-level ratings for each competency.

Common Interviewing Mistakes

1. **Relying on First Impressions:** Interviewers tend to make rapid decisions about the qualifications of a candidate within the first few minutes of the interview based on minimal information. Interviewers should reserve their judgment until sufficient information on the candidate has been gathered.

2. **Negative Emphasis:** Unfavorable information tends to be more influential and memorable than favorable information. Interviewers should avoid focusing on negative information to the exclusion of positive information.

3. **Not Knowing the Job:** Interviewers who do not have a comprehensive understanding of the skills needed for the job often form their own opinion about what constitutes the best candidate. They use this personal impression to evaluate candidates. Therefore, it is important to make sure interviewers fully understand the requirements of the job.

4. **Pressure to Hire:** When interviewers believe they need to make a decision quickly, they tend to make decisions based on a limited sample of information, or on a small number of candidate interviews. Interviewers should adhere to the established interview procedure and timeline with each candidate to avoid making erroneous decisions.

5. **Contrast Effects:** The order in which the candidates are interviewed can affect the ratings given to candidates. While making ratings, interviewers should refrain from comparing and contrasting candidates to those who have been previously interviewed.

6. **Nonverbal Behavior:** Interviewers should base their evaluation of the candidate on the candidate's past performance and current behavior as it relates to the competency being evaluated and ***not*** just on how the candidate acts during the interview. Questions and probes relating to the competencies of interest will usually direct the interviewer to the important information.

Appendix G: Sample Structured Interview Individual Rating Form

GENERAL COMPETENCIES:
The proficiency-level behavioral examples illustrate the types of behavior associated with each proficiency level, across the full range of HR functions. They are only examples, and candidates may demonstrate proficiency through behaviors not listed.

Writing: Recognizes or uses correct English grammar, punctuation, and spelling; communicates information (e.g., facts, ideas, or messages) in a succinct and organized manner; produces written information, which may include technical material that is appropriate for the intended audience.

Proficiency Rating (choose only one)	Proficiency Level Definition	Proficiency Level Behavioral Examples for Typical HR Positions
☐ 1	The candidate can apply the competency in the simplest situations. The candidate requires close and extensive guidance.	• Accurately copies information from one source to another. • Composes basic memos and emails. • Completes standard forms such as training forms and travel orders.
☐ 2	The candidate can apply the competency in somewhat difficult situations. The candidate will require frequent guidance.	• Assists in developing training materials for managers and employees. • Writes responses to non-selected job applicants. • Writes congratulatory letter to award recipients.
☐ 3	The candidate can apply the competency in difficult situations. The candidate may require occasional guidance.	• Proofreads internal memos for format and grammatical, spelling, and typographical errors. • Prepares informational material to communicate a new leave policy to employees. • Prepares a flowchart of the organization's hiring process. • Develops recruitment materials for a job fair.
☐ 4	The candidate can apply the competency in considerably difficult situations. The candidate requires no guidance.	• Writes a handbook for employees to describe HR procedures. • Prepares correspondence on a sensitive discipline case. • Prepares a position paper to defend a controversial HR program. • Prepares organization's written comments on proposed classification standards.
☐ 5	The candidate can apply the competency in exceptionally difficult situations. The candidate has served as a key resource and advised others.	• Writes the organization's strategic human capital plan. • Authors an article about the organization's innovative HR practices. • Develops legislative proposals to resolve critical HR issues affecting the organization's ability to achieve its mission.

Oral Communication: Expresses information (e.g., ideas or facts) to individuals or groups effectively, taking into account the audience and nature of the information (e.g., technical, sensitive, controversial); makes clear and convincing oral presentations; listens to others, attends to nonverbal cues, and responds appropriately.

Proficiency Rating (choose only one)	Proficiency Level Definition	Proficiency Level Behavioral Examples for Typical HR Positions
☐ 1	The candidate can apply the competency in the simplest situations. The candidate requires close and extensive guidance.	• Explains procedures for changing a beneficiary. • Refers prospective applicants to organization's website. • Responds to customer inquiries about pay schedules.
☐ 2	The candidate can apply the competency in somewhat difficult situations. The candidate will require frequent guidance.	• Reports on project status during weekly team meetings. • Explains special pay rate eligibility criteria to employees. • Presents information about flexible work schedules at new employee orientation. • Conducts exit interviews.
☐ 3	The candidate can apply the competency in difficult situations. The candidate may require occasional guidance.	• Describes the organization's employee assistance program to groups within the HR community. • Presents a summary of new regulations affecting the organization's mission at a staff meeting. • Responds to position classification inquiries from managers who are posting vacancies. • Describes new HR services to managers.
☐ 4	The candidate can apply the competency in considerably difficult situations. The candidate requires no guidance.	• Facilitates focus groups to elicit feedback on proposed performance management system. • Presents controversial decisions about organizational restructuring to employee groups. • Explains complicated new pay regulations to a lay group. • Explains to recruiters the impact of a legal decision on application procedures.
☐ 5	The candidate can apply the competency in exceptionally difficult situations. The candidate has served as a key resource and advised others.	• Presents controversial workforce diversity findings and recommendations to management. • Testifies about the organization's selection procedures at administrative proceedings. • Informs management of their misinterpretation of the Americans with Disabilities Act and recommends corrective action.

Problem Solving: Identifies problems; determines accuracy and relevance of information; uses sound judgment to generate and evaluate alternatives, and to make recommendations.

Proficiency Rating (choose only one)	Proficiency Level Definition	Proficiency Level Behavioral Examples for Typical HR Positions
☐ 1	The candidate can apply the competency in the simplest situations. The candidate requires close and extensive guidance.	• Corrects simple problems with Health Benefits Election forms. • Identifies missing training forms from personnel files. • Reviews information justifying employee award nominations for completeness.
☐ 2	The candidate can apply the competency in somewhat difficult situations. The candidate will require frequent guidance.	• Determines the appropriate changes to employees' official personnel folders in cases of marriage or divorce. • Recommends options for an employee who has no accrued annual or sick leave and is adopting a child. • Suggests review process for vacancy announcements to improve accuracy and clarity.
☐ 3	The candidate can apply the competency in difficult situations. The candidate may require occasional guidance.	• Resolves classification issues by researching precedent-setting case decisions. • Analyzes relevant information to identify barriers preventing participation in a mentoring program. • Applies pay rules and regulations to resolve a pay-setting dispute for a new employee.
☐ 4	The candidate can apply the competency in considerably difficult situations. The candidate requires no guidance.	• Integrates a variety of strategic hiring flexibilities to address recruitment and retention problems. • Identifies the immediate training needs of employees to address customer complaints. • Resolves union concerns about inconsistent performance ratings across the organization by implementing mandatory supervisory training.
☐ 5	The candidate can apply the competency in exceptionally difficult situations. The candidate has served as a key resource and advised others.	• Analyzes and solves complex labor-management disagreements involving vague and untested areas of case law regarding working conditions. • Resolves logistical problems associated with hiring several thousand employees to meet a temporary staffing need. • Resolves projected shortages in critical occupations by developing a comprehensive recruitment program to include outreach, mentoring, internships, and financial incentives.

Interpersonal Skills: Shows understanding, friendliness, courtesy, tact, empathy, concern, and politeness to others; develops and maintains effective relationships with others; may include effectively dealing with individuals who are difficult, hostile, or distressed; relates well to people from varied backgrounds and different situations; is sensitive to cultural diversity, race, gender, disabilities, and other individual differences.

Proficiency Rating (choose only one)	Proficiency Level Definition	Proficiency Level Behavioral Examples for Typical HR Positions
☐ 1	The candidate can apply the competency in the simplest situations. The candidate requires close and extensive guidance.	• Greets job applicants when they arrive for interviews. • Works with others in the HR office to organize information materials for employee orientation sessions.
☐ 2	The candidate can apply the competency in somewhat difficult situations. The candidate will require frequent guidance.	• Offers to assist employees in resolving problems with their benefits election. • Works with other HR staff on a cross-functional team to improve coordination of activities. • Works with others to minimize disruptions to an employee working under tight deadlines.
☐ 3	The candidate can apply the competency in difficult situations. The candidate may require occasional guidance.	• Restores a working relationship between angry co-workers who have opposing views. • Acts courteous and tactful when confronted by an employee who is frustrated by a payroll problem. • Establishes cooperative working relationships with managers, so they are comfortable asking for advice on HR issues.
☐ 4	The candidate can apply the competency in considerably difficult situations. The candidate requires no guidance.	• Facilitates an open forum to discuss employee concerns regarding new compensation system. • Maintains contact with stakeholder groups when implementing new employee development program. • Builds on the ideas of others to foster cooperation during bargaining agreement negotiations. • Identifies and emphasizes common goals to promote cooperation between HR and line staff. • Identifies and alleviates sources of stress among a team developing a new automated HR system.
☐ 5	The candidate can apply the competency in exceptionally difficult situations. The candidate has served as a key resource and advised others.	• Presents shortcomings of a newly installed HR automation system in a tactful manner to irate senior management officials. • Explains the benefits of controversial policy changes to upset individuals at a public hearing. • Diffuses an emotionally charged meeting with external stakeholders by expressing empathy for their concerns.

FINAL RATING

Candidate:_____ **Rater:**_____

General Competencies:	Proficiency Level
1. Writing	
2. Oral Communication	
3. Problem Solving	
4. Interpersonal Skills	

ACTION:

☐ Highly Recommended for Position

☐ Recommended for Position

☐ Not Recommended for Position

Interviewer's Signature: _____

Date: _____

Appendix H: Sample Structured Interview Group Rating Form

Candidate Name:			Date of Interview:	

Instructions: Transfer each interviewer's competency ratings onto this form. A consensus discussion must occur with each panel member justifying his or her rating. Any changes to the individual ratings during consensus discussion should be initialed by the panel members. A final group consensus rating must be entered for each competency.

Competency	Panelists' Individual Ratings			Consensus Group Rating
	(1)	(2)	(3)	
Writing				
Oral Communication				
Problem Solving				
Interpersonal Skills				

COMMENTS:

Name of Panel Chairperson #1 :

Name of Panel Member #2:

Name of Panel Member #3: